WHAT'S IN YOUR HAND, MR. PRESTON?

SHEILA BLACKMON-NEAL

Kingdom Builders Publications LLC

© 2021 Sheila Blackmon-Neal
What's in Your Hand, Mr. Preston?
Special Edition
Kingdom Builders Publications, LLC

All rights reserved. No part of this book may be reproduced or transmitted in any form or by any means without written permission from the author.

Printed in the USA

ISBN: 978-0-578-82932-6 Soft Cover
ISBN: 237-0-000-85565-7 Hard Cover Special Edition
Library of Congress Control Number

Authored by
Sheila Blackmon-Neal

Editor
Dr. Lakisha S. Forrester
Kingdom Builders Publications

Cover Design
LoMar Designs

Illustrator
Eric F. Quzack

This Book belongs to

DEDICATION

This book is dedicated to my grandchildren, Ashton, JaNya, Brayden, Carmen, Preston, and to those who will proceed them down to a thousand generations.

To all of my great nieces and great nephews, who were too young to remember my dad, your great-grandfather, I dedicate this book to you also! **What's In Your Hand, Mr. Preston?** should give each of you vision and insight on how great of a man he was.

I can only ask that you give me a solemn promise that this book will be read, shared, remembered, treasured, and passed down to the next generation! Also, promise me when you complete this book, you will acquire a copy of **The Life & Times of Rev. Dr. Preston Blackmon.** You will not regret it!!

ACKNOWLEDGMENTS

In writing this book, surprisingly and unknowingly, I have some of the same gifts my dad had. Our gifts are, but not limited to, artist/designer, singer/songwriter, basketball player, creator/inventor, writer/poet, preacher/pastor, and teacher. And we both were students at South Carolina State University. How unique is that?

In reading this book, you will discover Mr. Preston had many gifts. How about you? How many gifts do you have? Whether it's one or two, cherish, nurture, perfect, and thank God for each one. Mr. Preston used all of his, to the best of his ability.

In writing this book, I want to acknowledge my Heavenly Father, the Gift-Giver, who allowed me to possess so many gifts. The Book of James, Chapter 1, verse 17 (New King James Version) declares, "Every good gift and every perfect gift is from above, and comes down from the Father of lights, with whom there is no variation or shadow of turning." The Message Bible says, "Every desirable and beneficial gift comes out of heaven. The gifts are rivers of light cascading down from the Father of Light." And to my earthly dad, Mr. Preston, thanks for passing every 'good and perfect' gift you gave to me. I feel blessed and highly favored.

Sheila Blackmon-Neal

INTRODUCTION

This book is about Mr. Preston (Rev. Dr. Preston Blackmon). A gifted, skilled, talented, and unselfish man who shared every gift that he had with his God, his family, and all of mankind. Especially to the citizens of Lancaster, South Carolina.

What's In Your Hand, Mr. Preston? is a book that depicts a man who used his hands to build, create, and teach. He used his mind to further his education to become a teacher, preacher, constable, and city councilman. Lastly, Mr. Preston used his heart as a servant, a missionary, a caregiver, a spokesman, an advocate, and a leader in his community, town, and state.

Mr. Preston survived the odds, overcoming many adversities in his life. He had dreams and visions to succeed at every and anything he assigned his head, hands, and heart to. He also had faith in God to know all things were possible.

May this book encourage you as a young reader to surpass the odds, circumstances, and difficulties life may bring. May this book encourage you to soar, dream big, finish strong, and use whatever is in your hand which God gave you to glorify Him. He is the Gift-Giver.

When you finish reading this book, read my second book, **The Life & Times of Rev. Dr. Preston Blackmon.** Visit the website:

http://prestonblackmoncenter.org Google the city of Lancaster, South Carolina and read about The Preston Blackmon Southside Park in the Southside Community.

"What's in your hand, Mr. Preston?"

"A basketball!"

"Why a basketball?"

"It is one of my favorite sports. It kept me fit and in good shape."

Mr. Preston was a member of the Mighty Five as a basket ball player.

"What's in your hand, Mr. Preston?"

"A notepad!"

"Why a notepad?"

"So I can promote justice as a police officer."

Mr. Preston was the first African American police officer in the city of Lancaster, SC in 1960.

"What's in your hand, Mr. Preston?"

"A ticket!"

"Why a ticket?"

"I have to write tickets to remind citizens to uphold the law."

Mr. Preston was a constable for the city of Lancaster, SC.

"What's in your hand, Mr. Preston?"

"A brick and a masonry trowel!"

"Why a brick and a trowel?"

"They are instruments I use to build brick walls."

Mr. Preston was a successful brick masonry Contractor for many years. He even built his own home and church.

"What's in your hand, Mr. Preston?"

"A saw!"

"Why a saw?"

"So I can cut the wooden pieces I need to assemble my work."

Mr. Preston was a master builder who loved to cut, create, and assemble things.

"What's in your hand, Mr. Preston?"

"A compass and calculator!"

"Why a compass and calculator?"

"These are tools I need to complete my class assignments."

Mr. Preston was a keen math student.

"What's in your hand, Mr. Preston?"

"A book!"

"Why a book?"

"Because going to school and getting a good education are important."

Mr. Preston believed education is the key to success and knowledge is power.

He was a brick masonry teacher at Barr Street High School, Lancaster, SC.

"What's in your hand, Mr. Preston?"

"A pool stick!"

"Why a pool stick?"

"So I can challenge my opponents in a game of billiards."

Mr. Preston was a spectacular billiard player.

"What's in your hand, Mr. Preston?"

"A steering wheel!"

"Why a steering wheel?"

"So I can steer my way around the neighborhood to pick up children to ride my bus to school."

Mr. Preston was a school bus driver for the public schools.

"What's in your hand, Mr. Preston?"

"A briefcase!"

"Why a briefcase."

"It is used to contain all of my notes for the city meetings."

Mr. Preston was a city councilman who loved the city of Lancaster, South Carolina.

"What's in your hand, Mr. Preston?"

"A Bible!"

"Why a Bible?"

"To preach the Word of God to all who would hear."

Mr. Preston was an ordained minister and pastor.

"What's in your hand, Mr. Preston?"

"A hymn book!"

"Why a hymn book?"

"So I can sing praises unto God. It gives my heart joy."

Mr. Preston was a talented singer and songwriter.

"What's in your hand, Mr. Preston?"

"Someone else's hand!"

"Why is that Mr. Preston?"

"For so many reasons,

I always believed if I could help someone or cheer someone,

then my living will not be in vain."

Mr. Preston was a servant to all of mankind.

MR PRESTON'S DICTIONARY

BASKETBALL PLAYER. An individual who uses a basketball and a goal to score points in an indoor gym or outdoor court.

BILLIARDS PLAYER. A player who uses a long stick to hit balls in the side and corner pockets on a large table.

BRICK MASONRY CONTRACTOR. A person who is hired to perform duties with bricks, such as building a house, fireplaces, and/or walls.

BUILDER. An individual who builds, assembles, and constructs with various materials.

CITY COUNCILMAN. A person who is a member of a council that represents a city. They help establish laws and ordinances for the city at large.

CONSTABLE. A public figure who is hired like a police officer to assist in upholding the law.

ORDAINED MINISTER & PASTOR. Ministers preach the gospel, the Word of God. A pastor is an overseer over a church and a body of people to build the Kingdom of God.

POLICE OFFICER. A male or a female on a police force. They perform duties that consists of enforcing laws, investigate crimes, and making arrests.

SCHOOL BUS DRIVER. A person who is certified to drive a public school bus to transport students from their homes to their schools.

SERVANT. A person who volunteers or is paid to serve others.

SINGER. A person who sings alone, with a band, or a choir.

STUDENT. An individual who is enrolled in a public or private school, college, or university to further their education.

TEACHER. A certified instructor who teaches students from various learning materials for educational purposes.

ABOUT THE AUTHOR

Rev. Sheila Blackmon-Neal – Born the seventh child of the late Rev. Dr. Preston and Wilma Myers Blackmon and the widow of the late Deacon William G. Neal. After graduating from Lancaster High School, Lancaster, South Carolina in 1975, Rev. Neal enrolled at Allen University, majoring in Art Education. In the fall of 1977, Rev. Neal transferred from Allen University to South Carolina State University, earning a Bachelor of Science degree in Art Education in December 1980.

Rev. Neal furthered her studies in Art Education, earning a Masters of Education degree from Cambridge College, Cambridge, Massachusetts (1998). After accepting the call into ministry, she earned a Masters of Divinity and Theology from Beacon University, Macon Georgia (2007).

In 2014, Rev. Neal retired as a public school teacher with 32 years of experience. Presently, she lives in Lancaster, but pastors the One Step Christian Ministries, Inc., in Bishopville, South Carolina.

Rev. Neal is grateful to God for allowing her to write this memoir about her dad. She gives Him praise and glory.

www.ingramcontent.com/pod-product-compliance
Lightning Source LLC
Chambersburg PA
CBHW081157290426
44108CB00018B/2581